Introduction

Welcome to my first collection of poems.

The words in my mind.

You will be coming on the journey with me through my poems; I wanted to share this to show my journey through mental health, loss, bullying and much more.

Through my work I hope you will feel connections with my experiences and see that anything is possible.

I never thought I would be sharing this with anyone, but I am so glad you are reading these words.

Remember whatever life throws at you, never give up.

J W Wright

Index

Anxiety

As anxiety takes hold

As my mind and soul go cold

As dreams and hopes die

Drowned in the tears I cry

Falling like leaves from the tree

No longer ahead can I see

Only the past like a beast at my heels

As it rips away joy and happiness it steals

You find out who does really care

Who will always be there

And who is like the sun

When the darkness comes they run

But the ones who ran, that hurt so much more

The ones who slammed the door

The only mistake made, one so strong and just

Was to let them in and give them your trust

For they didn't care for you for a second

The moment a life without you beckoned

Stand up tall and brush yourself off and then

Remember I am so much better than them

Maybe one day they will be in need and in pain

They will need a friend, an umbrella in hells rain

Maybe then they will know the pain dealt

Maybe then they will know the pain I felt

A world without you

In this world nothing is set in stone

Our souls from heaven merely on loan

But everything in life happens for a reason

No matter the weather no matter the season

You came into my life at the right time

Right when I thought it was the end of the line

Right when the moon would fall from my sky

When I just thought I wanted to die

You changed everything the world no longer hostile

My sadness began to turn to a smile

The seasons change the clock ticks on

I could not imagine my life if you were gone

If in the world you were no longer here

The boat of my life would no longer steer

I pray you are always there

The heart and kindness you have is so rare

It maybe selfish but I want you in my life forever

With you there I can face every endeavour

You encourage me and give me strength

No matter the pain or times length

I can not imagine my life without you my friend

Right to times very end

The person who gives me heart to pull through

And most of all I can not imagine a world with out you

The day I lost you

The days and months pass so fast

The world before me beautiful and vast

I go through life thinking you will always be there

Maybe God could have answered my prayer

As time ticks on and summer becomes winter

Even the strongest trees one day will splinter

We can not stop the call of time

Every mountain we can not climb

When we were young and free we could never be told

That one day we would become old

Do not let time pass you by

Swim in the rivers before they dry

Follow your hopes and dreams

As life is not as long as it seems

Make time for family and friends before time moves on

Because one day they will be gone

Life is for love and laughter

Not sitting and waiting for the hereafter

As the clock of life never stops

The leaves from the tree always drops

But as the dark clouds roll in

The winter of life does begin

We will always have memories of the past

The time in life travelled so fast

As I grow old the people I cared for have gone away

I wish they had been here to stay

Time should be well spent, that I knew

But the worst day is when I lost you

Never forget me

When my clock of life ticks no more

When I close my mortal door

When my flowing river runs dry

When the angels begin to cry

I hope you will remember me

Look to the stars and you will see

Even though I am no longer here, I will always remember you

To watch over and guide you through

When the angels took me to heaven above

I left you my hope, I left you my love

When I fall from life's great tree

I hope you will remember me

I hope someone will cry for me

When the angels set my soul free

When I am with my family in heaven above

And leave behind those that I love

Please remember you are always in my heart

No matter how long we are apart

Remember when life is hard with no way through

I am there and will always love you

When life is tough and filled with fear

I love you and I am always near

Remember when I fell from life's tree

I will never forget you, please never forget me

The day time stopped

The day you left me, the day you went

I screamed to the world I do not consent

The day you left my whole world dropped

This is the day time stopped

The day an angel took you under her wing

The day the choir did no longer sing

The day that put a hole in my heart

The day my life fell apart

You were my world, you were my sun

The world was cold and drained of fun

Why did you leave me, I did cry

Why did you go, why did you die

Without you I have lost all hope

Without you can I can not cope

But then the angel came down from high

Wings so grand they blocked the sky

She said to me if they are in your heart

You will never truly be apart

They will always be with you from above in the sky

Always remember them but do not cry

When your time here is done

They will descend from heaven beyond the sun

They will hold you and take your hand

To take you back to their beautiful land

Where the sky is filled with magnificent light

A place no longer filled with night

But remember when your soul dropped

Will be the day for another loved one, the day that time stopped

Fallen Leaves

Fluttering down from all around

Scattering lifelessly across the ground

In the tree of our own birth

We wait to fall and return to the earth

We climb the branch to reach the sky

But in the end we wither and die

We try to control all around

But in the end we fall to the ground

Be we rich, be we poor

In a hut or a house of grandeur

In the end we are all the same

To return to the place from which we came

We fight and strive to reach the sun

As the road to the end has begun

Care for those for whom you love

Rather than the riches above

Treasure your friends, family and mind

As in the end you will find

That as the tree of life breaths

We are all but fallen leaves

My ocean

When the storm of my minds emotion

Come and goes like the waves of my ocean

When I feel the boat of my life is about to sink

The moment I begin to overthink

The waves crashing on my soul

The moment I loose my control

I stand still, it feels so remote

Like a single thing will sink my boat

I feel so lost at sea

Like I have lost a piece of me

Lost and afraid in my ocean

Moving along in my minds motion

A boat in my mind with no way off

No lifeboat to castoff

No anchor to keep me still

So lost I begin to loose will

But in the distance I see a light

Pushing through the darkest night

And from the light comes a hand

Getting me up and to the land

When you are in the storm and rain

Spinning round your on brain

Do not give up because you will find

A person in your life who is so kind

The hand in the night

To give you the strength to fight

To hold your hand and give you the notion

To break free from your minds ocean

The garden

There is sits filled with flowers and trees

I sit and listen to the buzzing of bees

I let the sun bath my face

I am here in my happy place

My mind is calm and at peace

The horrible thoughts they begin to cease

Is this how it felt at my birth?

At one with the garden and the earth

To relax and feel so calm

That I can come to no harm

No more ticking of my minds clock

My thoughts they no longer flock

Take my time to unwind

To make time for me to find

To have peace in my mind and heart

Before everything begins to start

Find that moment to step away

For a minute for a day

You are kind and have a beautiful soul

Always find time to take back what sadness stole

Time to heal and time to mend

Time for you to spend

When you feel you are done

Spend that time in the garden

The island

A silent island in the middle of a calm see

A place in this world just for me

A tranquil and wonderful place

Where I can sit with the sun in my face

A place where I can get away from life's fate

To take a break and let the whole world wait

A place to relax and unwind

To calm my state of mind

A place to sit with coffee or wine

A place that is all mine

As you listen to your music play

Let your troubles drift away

Make that time and place just for you

It will help you get through

All the things that life throws

What is around the corner no one knows

Look after your heart, look after your soul

And you can achieve any goal

To yourself be kind

Look after your own mind

Your heart so big and soul so bright

You are a beacon, you are a light

It always looks after you

And you will always make it through

My minds fire

Like a burning in my head

Like a book that remains unread

Like the end of the world entire

Inside my minds fire

The beat of an angel's wing

The crown from a fallen king

Like I am trapped in mire

Inside my minds fire

My heart burned and hurt

Trapped in my minds desert

My negative thoughts get higher and higher

Inside my minds fire

Everything in life I begin to doubt

I can find no way out

No happy thought I can acquire

Inside my minds fire

How do I put this fire out?

When I am empty throughout

No call of angel, no song of a choir

Inside my minds fire

Do not hope for the end

Reach out for a friend

They are the call of an angel; they are the voice of the choir

To help you put out my minds fire

Not enough time

Not enough time in the world

Yet everything before you is unfurled

Not enough time in the day

Remember nothing is here to stay

Make time for family and friends

We never know when the curtain descends

But always make time just for you

When the clock stops we do not have a clue

Do what makes you happy and fills you with joy

Baking, writing or just a new toy

Go where you want as much as you can

Do not put off every plan

Go with your loved ones or friends you hold dear

Whether you travel far or just somewhere near

Walk along beaches in day's late embrace

Or sit in the morning waiting for the sun on your face

Spend the time with those who love you my dear

Sit in the garden drinking Pinna Colada or beer

And those you have not seen for many a night

When you see them hug them so tight

Remember we can fill our lives with what we love so

Do not let the time in your life drift past and go

The next time they say not enough time

Remind them that wasting what we have is such a crime

The birds of love

When the suns rises just over the hills

And the birds dance on your window sills

When the sun beams through like a fire

And the birds sing their morning choir

You look to window after your rest

Watching you, a robin red breast

Flying away towards the sun

You smile, could be your dad or your mum

Come to check me to be sure I am fine

Their love for you so divine

You leave your home and down the lane

The flowers and trees like natures frame

The bird's morning song fills the air

Days like this are so very rare

You look to the skies to see the birds above

Each one carrying you hopes and love

You walk past some houses all in a row

Stood on the path before you sat an old crow

Looked at me slowly and gave me a wink

Like an old friend I am began to think

Suddenly a sound from up on high

I saw a flock of doves in the sky

These mornings they warm my heart

I can not wait for the next one to start

I feel I can face every one of life's tests

Then stood before two robin red breasts

Smiled to myself, hello mum and dad

For the birds of love I am ever so glad

The river

The river turns, the river bends

No one really knows where it ends

Some people say it flows to the deep blue sea

But I know it flows from you to me

Along the banks of the river lay beautiful flowers and trees

As you pass through time just seems to freeze

As you drift slowly towards the sun

You realise you are not the only one

The river is covered in beautiful boats

Each filled with love and hopes

As I drift so slowly near

A voice I know I begin to hear

As I draw close I see the shore

Scattered in shadows I see before

As my boats rests on the sand

Reached out before me a loving hand

As I look up to see the face of my mum

She smiles and says welcome my beautiful one

I look beyond her I see all those in life who passed

What about the ones I left behind I asked

She smiled and said do not worry my dear

When their time comes you will be here

To greet them from their journey, to reach out your hand

Help them from their boat to the sand

All those you leave you will see some day

When they reach the river when they have passed away

You will be here to see all you love

To take their hand and lead them to heaven above

The journey

In the early morning dawn

I am up before night has withdrawn

Pack my bag upon my back

Step through the gate onto the track

I walk the track to the river

Do my coat up as I feel a shiver

I follow the river to a lake

Where I sit and take a break

I follow the winding track up the hill

The world is calm, the world is still

I climb the hill and reach the top

Where I see the whole world and stop

Down the other side I see a mist

Yet the sun my cheek it just kissed

As I walk down to the unknown

I suddenly feel no longer alone

As I reach the bottom I see a town

With lots of people all around

Faces of people from my past

All the people in my life who have passed

My family, my pets and my friend

All in the past I could depend

I look at my watch and it just reads eleven

I know where I am, I am in heaven

Paw prints

From the stumble in a kittens walk

To teaching a young puppy to talk

They bring you happiness they bring you joy

From their cuddles to playing with their first toy

As they grow they take a place in your very soul

They love you dearly your very heart they have stole

Your very family they have become

In their innocent eyes you are their dad or their mum

You love them always and worry when their ill

No matter what they love you still

If you leave them for a week or just a day

You miss them in every way

Weather you play with them on the floor

Or just sit there and hold their paw

Their love for you never ending

Heal your heart when it is bending

And when the day comes their no longer here

Remember one thing and never fear

Before the tears begin to start

That they will forever leave paw prints on you heart

Heavens gate

To my family and my friends who I hold dear

I need to make one thing very clear

When I am old and grey

When the angels have taken you away

When they take you to heaven on high

When all I can do is cry

Please for me just wait

Wait for me at heavens gate

I would be here on my own

But when the angel comes, I do not want to walk into heaven alone

I want you there to hold my hand

And take me into heavens wonderful land

I know when you go; my tears will cause a flood

I will feel pain through my soul into my very blood

But I will not be long in this state

Knowing you will wait for me at heavens gate

Stars

Like a billion souls watching down on me

Shinning in the sky for all to see

Mothers and fathers watching their children grow

Watching them live their lives below

Look up to see your mum and dad

Looking after you through good and bad

The shine of their star

Shows how proud they are

To see how far you have come

Far from the place you came from

They are so proud of who you are

Remember this when you see their star

They are always with you

Their love for you always true

They are in you soul and your heart

From you they are never apart

Their love for you is so divine

They love you as long as the stars shine

Always at your side

To comfort you when you cried

Look up to the stars to see them smile

Remember them for a while

Their love for you is true

Remember you miss them and they miss you too

Sparkles in the sand

The sun beams down on a golden sea

Lighting the horizon as far as the quay

I take a deep breath and think of the words

As I look to the sky and watch the birds

I stand and look down the empty beach

As the seagulls begin to screech

I look around and see not a single soul

As I walk along on my lonely stroll

The water laps my toes

As the world around me slows

I stop to look to the skies

But the sun just hurts my eyes

As I walk for what seems like days

Under the suns golden gaze

The sun gentle warms my skin

It calms my soul within

I stop and watch the tide alone

Like a king sat on an empty throne

No golden crown on his head

No idea what lies ahead

Towards the end I reach a pier

A voice in the distance I begin to hear

I stop and stare, I begin to listen

As the sand before me begins to glisten

I turn to see your beautiful face

No longer alone in this wonderful place

As I turn to you to take your hand

I realise we are just sparkles in the sand

Tides of infinity

As the sun rises above the dunes

Waves galloping like White horses

Crashing into the shore

Washing my soul to the very core

Washing away my dreams

Nothing as it seems

As waters rise and fall

As they answer natures call

As waves rise and crash

Against my heart the waters bash

Waters give life and take it away

But on the sandy shore I stay

Tides sweep away my love

Take them to the sky above

Tides like time passing by

As blue and dangerous as the sky

As I stand facing the sea

Rolling in like demons crest

Time ebbs away like water through my hand

With smiling face, here I stand

The tides grow, rising above the sun

I wait to be consumed I can not run

The waters of time I have affinity

As I watch the tides of infinity

Time

Flying by like a shooting star

Stealing moments we put off till tomorrow

Before we know we have travelled so far

Before we know it, tomorrow is yesterday

Today has gone and tomorrow is today

Plans put off drift away in the mists of time

Before we know it, arrives the end of the line

Don't put off what you can do today

As time moves on, nothing will stay

Cherish your family, your friends so true

Before time crashes like a wave

Taking away all you could have done

To all my family and friends so dear

I love you all, that much is clear

Never put off making memories too long

As time flows on, one day they will be gone

Make time for family and friends

Make that trip, see that dream

Before the sands of time swallow all that could have been

The world stopped turning

To the first person to break my heart

On the day you left me there

The day you said you did not care

You said you never loved me

Walked away, so you could be free

Smashed my heart like a cheap vase

Turned away and broke your gaze

I was just a toy to throw away

You had no wish to stay

Built me up like I was a king

Made me feel I could sing

But cruelty was your wish

Revenge on a cold dish

But revenge for another man

To hurt me instead was the plan

You would make me feel loved

But into my heart a knife shoved

Made me feel I was worthless and weak

For years love I did not seek

Walked away while my life was burning

While the world stopped turning

My heart did not wish to beat anymore

As I laid there on the floor

You moved on after the damage was done

What pain did you feel, none

I did not trust anyone for such a long time

I felt like being in love again was a crime

No matter the damage you did to my mind

I am better than you, I am always kind….

The rains come

Music on glass roofs

Deluge from above

Masking the sun

When the rains come

Winds breathe blows

As the rains come

Clouds gather in groups

As the waters run

Music on glass roofs

Deluge from above

Hides the face of the sun

When the rains come

The finger of god

Pointing the way

Leading to the day

The day you left me

The day your soul set free

All that remains is the thought of you

A picture in my mind, to get me through

Memories are all that remain

No day will ever be the same

I loved you with all my heart

Right from the very start

Now you fade away like a ghost

And what I miss the most

I miss your laugh, your beautiful smile

The kindness to sit with me for a while

Now I am alone, I miss you so

I know it was time, but why did you go

I will remember you till my last day

You are always with me, even if you didn't stay

I will miss you, every second I remain

I will cry tears like rain

You will live on in my heart and mind

You were so wonderful, so kind

You always helped me through

But most of all, I will always miss you

Rainbows end

Red is the sky, in early morning light

Orange are the leaves, as birds take flight

Yellow the sun burns high above

Green the grass that grows tended with love

Blue the sky as the rains come

Indigo the flowers that grow

Violet the seeds we sow

When to heavens garden I tend

I will meet you at rainbows end

Chains

My brain so heavy if feels wrapped in chains

The reason for all of my life's pains

Years of not knowing who I am or what to do

Not even fight to pull me through

Being tormented for being who I am

Made to feel my life was a scam

Just because I was quiet and mild

They chose to destroy my inner child

As the years went by the chains grew heavy

Like a ledger that would not levy

I carried them all alone

Until they wore my hands to the bone

I lost a childhood I never knew

Felt like a hole in my heart punched through

The flowers in my life only watered in tears

Every dream destroyed by fears

In life I didn't feel I did belong

Like a choir missing a song

I felt so unhappy and alone

I didn't even feel I deserved a home

Bullies don't have to deal with their action

The pain I carry they wouldn't know a fraction

They continue their lives like a new start

While mine just starts to fall apart

I cried myself to sleep every night

I lost the Will, I was losing the fight

All I wanted was a friend to hug me

To tell me everything was to be alright and make me see

That the world isn't just filled with pain and hate

My life before me wasn't just a locked gate

To help me carry the heavy chains of my mind

So in life I could find

Friendship, happiness and the will to go on

The road I travelled alone for so long

So If I open my heart to you please be aware

To trust anyone in my life is very rare

Why I shared my heart and pain will become so clear

Because I finally found someone I trust and hold dear

The chains in my mind are still there

But now they feel as light as air

I still sometimes have a bad day

But I have a friend in my life to say

If the bad times come or when it rains

I am there to help carry the chains

I travelled so long on life's road

But now to me you have showed

I no longer need to travel it alone

I have my family, my wife and I am home

Always

A poem for the true friend I hope is out there one day.

Through life's storms and rain

Through your happiness and pain

Through life's walkways

I will be by your side always

With every twist and every turn

With every single life's concern

I will be there all days

By your side always

With every tear that falls

I will help you over life's walls

When you come to life's crossways

I will be there for you always

When you feel alone

Trapped in life's cyclone

If you feel trapped in a maze

I will be there always

Your friend until the very stars fade

To hold your hand if your afraid

To give you comfort, to give you praise

I am your friend always

You are my family, you are my friend

Right to the very end

Even if the world was ablaze

You are my friend and I love always

Broken heart

Smashed on the rocks

Broken like a delicate vase

Lost in the dark maze

Of the hollow broken heart

You brushed me aside

Gave no reason, gave no cause

Deceived by the one I did confide

The broken pieces in my hand

I stare at you and wonder why

I gave my heart, gave my whole

But you abused and broke my soul

As you walk away, tears of pain I cry

Like sand running through fingers

The pain aches and lingers

Lost in the dark maze

Of the hollow broken heart

Architect of my destruction

Fire burns to the core

Ripping through my soul

Tearing dreams apart

As my will falls to the floor

Grasping at the door

Pulling down the walls

As my life falters and falls

As I fall into the pit

There I watch, there I sit

A witness to my own mind

A place of no construction

The architect of my destruction

Door to my heart

There is an old wooden door where it should not be

Hidden away so no one can see

I last used the key many years ago

Where it is now I do not know

If you knock the door no one will come

Just the distant sound of a beating drum

I want to open that door so much

Swing it wide and finally touch

The beating heart that sits inside

But I lost the key I cried

I love my family, my wife

What else is there in life?

But I know now in the end

The key to the lock is held by a friend

Because the key to the door heaven entrust

To a person kind, caring and just

You took my hand and led me before

The old decaying locked door

You stood with me and said I was your friend from the start

Our friendship is the key to the door in your heart...

A day in my mind

Welcome, please come in

Make yourself at home

Welcome to a day in my head

Filled with thoughts but always alone

Behind a mask of elegance

Face broken, streaked with tears

Heart pounding, haunted by fears

As flood gates open, thoughts rush in

Do you like me at all?

I hate me, I begin to fall

Everyone hates me

Better off if I set my soul free

One last breath, no one would care

Just point at me, laugh and stare

No one cares, no one loves me

What did I do wrong?

Should I end my life's song?

Time to sleep, in hope to never wake

My heart and mind forsake

Why do you hate me, what did I do

Please tell me I don't have a clue

As the thoughts begin to subside

As planets in my mind collide

I sit with head in hands

Wonder how I made it through

Heart rate slows, mind grow silent

Thoughts no longer cruel or violent

Calm, despite what my mind said

Welcome to a day in my head

Made it through, come what may

Until it all begins again the next day

So never judge, always be kind

Welcome to a day in my mind

There for you

As the time drifts by

As the birds of winter fly

As night follows day

I am here to stay

As true as the stars in the night

As wonderful as early mornings light

As kind as an angels wing

As gentle as the start of spring

You were there during the storm

With heart so kind, so warm

What ever the world brings around

No matter how loud the storms sound

I will be there for you my friend

Right till the world's very end

No matter what may come

Even if the darkness took the sun

I will be the light in the night

Be I near or out of sight

There for you all days

There for you, always

Worry storm

Let me take you to my minds skies

Only to show you the world through my eyes

Some days my mind is like a battling storm

Sometimes like an old tree withered and worn

I message you almost everyday

Not to annoy but to make sure you're ok

As it took me over forty years to find

Someone so gentle and so kind

Someone who looked passed my flaws

Someone I didn't repulse or give cause

To walk away like all others have done

To make me a world with no sun

I repeat myself only through worry

Like my mind is in a mad hurry

In the past I was tortured and hurt

And just shoved in the dirt

In the past so hard I have tried

But in the end I just stopped and cried

You are the first to see passed all this

To pull me back from the ends abyss

You have seen me through my worry storm

Your heart so kind, gentle and warm

But please remember in the end

I worry because I don't want to loose my friend

The valley

The mist rolls in down to the Brook

The valley sits before me like an open book

I see flowers stretched before me for miles

Covering the fields over the wooden styles

I see a cottage by a tiny stream

Where the sun light begins to gleam

Next to the cottage an oak tree stands tall

Surrounded by an tiny wall

As I get to the cottage I see a gate

A sign on it says only love no hate

I lift the latch and step right through

Where I am going o have not a clue

I feel the worlds weight lift from me

As I sit by the old oak tree

I look around and see people I used to know

Lost from my past where did they all go

Family, friends, all those I held dear

Where I was became ever so clear

On the ground before me lays a toy

Sat before me, my dog my lost little boy

Everything lost to me in life

My family, my pets and my loving wife

And my friend for me to hold

In a place I will never feel cold

A place I can walk through the paths and dales

Like a ship with a wind in its sails

Stood with my family and friends, the wind in my face

This is my heaven, my perfect place

Will you miss me

If the sun rose tomorrow and I was gone

Would you miss me?

If my clock stopped ticking and I was no more

If my face you could no longer see

Would you miss me if I left?

Would you miss me if I vanished without a trace?

If I never woke up again

If the sun no longer brushed my face

Would you think of me with happy thoughts?

Smile at the thought of the way I was

Laugh when you remember me

All this just because

I loved you with all my heart

My world was complete because of you

I may be gone but I am still here

To help you and guide you through

Will you miss me, as much as I miss you?

My heart no longer beats, but it stills holds on

To our memories, to our past

I may not be here, I may be gone

As I rose to the sky, I tried to hold on

But I lost my grip of your hand

As I left this world and drifted away from you

As lights went out and I could no longer stand

As darkness came down and I was gone

My love for you will always remain, I hope you see

I will miss you always my love

Will you miss me?

Hades fury

With anger like a storm of fire

Rage that would consume the world entire

The fires burn like the bowels of hell

As you fall deeper into that well

The red mist comes like a fog of hate

As you stand before hells gate

You loose control like a puppet of fear

The fire burning all those who are near

When the anger falls like meteor of rage

When the beast is set free from your minds cage

When your mind is out of your control

As you fall deeper into the hole

As you let the rage takes over your heart

It will slowly rip your soul apart

As you stand before your minds jury

Your world cracked by hades fury

The world keeps turning

What ever happens in life the world keeps turning

No matter how bad things seem, the fires keep burning

Even if you stopped the world would carry on

If you did not sing, there would still be a song

Do not sit down and hope for the end

Be yourself, you will find a friend

You may feel alone some days

You may feel hidden from the suns rays

You may want to step off the world as it turns

Jump into the fire that burns

But the world will carry on without you

There may be no light to see you through

But with family and friends we are complete

Feel we can again stand on our feet

Sometimes we are the puzzle just missing a piece

The volcano waiting to release

A friend is the missing pillar of my life

I have my family, my wife

But I was missing one final part

So in life I can again start

From a new beginning on a new road

With my family and friend to help with the load

How broken can a heart be, completely in the end

But with family, a true friend. In time it will mend

Wrong

Where did I go wrong?

How did I mess this up?

I can not face it again

Living life like an empty cup

I messed things up

How did I do this again?

I am like a broken umbrella

Smashed by the rain

How can I mess this up so bad?

I tried so hard and all to fail

I sit like broken glass

Smashed by life's hail

I can't wind the time back

I wish the friends I had stayed

Where did I go wrong?

With the mess I have made

Have I pushed my only friend away?

Please god don't let that be true

Because if I have, how I carry on

I don't have a clue

Hold my hand

Hold my hand son, I will guide you

Walk you through the world while you learn

Help you up when you fall down

Show you that in life some things you earn

Hold my hand son; let me show you the way

Let me help you make your own way in life

Through its hardships and its pain

Make your way through every strife

Hold my hand son, as time moves on

So you can stand on your own

As one day I will not be here

Knowing how much you have grown

Hold my hand son; it is not a strong as it was

As time has caught up with me

Made me old and frail my dear

I am so proud of you, I hope you see

I can not hold your hand son, as I am too weak

My clock is stopping, setting my sun

I reach out my hand and take hold

I will be your strength, hold my hand mum

The last staircase

On the last day I remember clear

Was a day filled with dread and fear

When you were weak and on the brink

The day I know my heart would sink

The day you breathed your last

Looking back the time went so fast

Before I knew it you were gone

The person I always relied upon

Taken too soon from my life's path

I miss your smile, I miss your laugh

You were the first friend I ever had

I thought my life would be forever sad

On the day the went up the last staircase

The last day I saw your face

But I know you sent to me

I locked my heart but you sent the key

I have a friend so true, so kind

That I know you sent them to find

My broken heart and help it heal

To make me smile and make me feel

You are still missed every day

But I thank you for my friend here to stay

You knew I was so alone, my heart smashed

But then like the heavens opened and the sun flashed

The most amazing person I could ever know

Who had a soul so kind it sparkled and did glow

Thank you for my friend, as you watch from space

The place you went on the last staircase

Cry

As the tears fall from the sky above

As I think of the people I love

As I think of the ones I have lost

How my life has changed, at what cost

I cry with happiness rather than pain

As they fall like heavens rain

Because to have them in my life was a blessing

My mind broken I was digressing

But worse would be to have never had them

So wonderful like a beautiful gem

My life so complete having known their soul

My life felt so whole

Sometimes tears are with joy of love

Not the loss of them to the sky above

The joy of knowing and loving someone so dear

That the world becomes so clear

You may miss them so much

Want to hold them and to touch

But to know they loved you as you loved them

Is like having them there again

Black notes

Ivory keys

Beautiful notes

Gentle tunes

In the air floats

Striking cords

Sings the choir

Pours the rain

Burns the fire

Dreams fall

Harmony floats

As in life's music

We all play black notes

Broken rhyme

Smashed and torn

Crumpled on the floor

Lost the will to fight

Closed every door

Rhymes that no longer work

The trees bend in the breeze

I stand back up bruised

I will not stop, never freeze

No more a broken rhyme

I will make it in time

Show those who doubt

I am me, I am now

I will be the one to show the world

I am good enough

I will write, they will listen

The journey before me unfurled

With help at my side

Strength in my heart

This is not the end

Merely the start